Special Days

Bilbo Books Publishing

ATHENS, GEORGIA

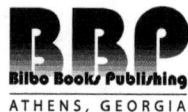

BBP
Bilbo Books Publishing
ATHENS, GEORGIA

bilbobooks.com

Table of Contents

Table of Contents

Special Days

Poetry by Alice L. Mohor

Illustrations by Carol J. Mohor

· 10 ·

Special Days

lest we forget
the reason why
someone somewhere
did loud decry

forever more
a day would be
set apart by
a grand decree

this poem book
is to recall
just why a day
might still enthrall

because we each
when made aware
will value and
more fully care

· 12 ·

Holidays

holidays once
were holy days
for sacrifice
penance or praise

worshipers were
bound together
by rituals
tied to weather

different from
impositions
we celebrate
new traditions

to remember
and honor past
beliefs and truths
we still hold fast

SUNDAY | MONDAY | TUESDAY | WEDNESDAY | THURSDAY | FRIDAY | SATURDAY

1 2 3 4 5 6
S P E C I A L
7 8 9 10 11 12 13
14 15 16 17 18 19 20
21 22 23 24 25 26 27
28 29 30 31

D A Y S

Written By: Alice L. Muhor

Illustrated by: Carol J. Muhor

Chapter One

National Holidays and Observances

• 16 •

New Year's Day

from long ago
superstitions
new year's day now
has traditions

resolutions
for better health
with black eyed peas
and greens for wealth

a holiday
to watch tv
floats of flowers
parades to see

college football
home teams to cheer
a happy way
to start the year

· 18 ·

Martin Luther King, Jr. Day

we celebrate
this man of worth
on a monday
close to his birth

we remember
his words so brave
from the speeches
he proudly gave

peaceful protest
his only choice
for equal rights
he gave loud voice

to honor him
service is done
to make our world
a peaceful one

·20·

Presidents' Day

washington fought
to make us free
from england's rule
of tyranny

our government's
first president
our country's grand
experiment

lincoln kept our
states together
the strife of war
beyond measure

a simple man
of complex worth
gave our nation
a second birth

Leap Day

earth's orbit 'round
our star the sun
is not exact
to how clocks run

to synchronize
our calendar
an extra day
needs to occur

three common years
and then a leap
so space and time
together keep

our shortest month
gets one more day
and some believe
girls have their say

•24•

Memorial Day

brave people fought
for our country
to make us safe
to keep us free

brave people died
for you and me
on land in air
and ocean sea

brave people gone
but not forgot
we decorate
each grave site plot

brave people now
are heroes made
from memory
must never fade

Flag Day

music lyrics
have proudly told
the story of
your colors bold

how people feel
when you march by
respect we show
when high you fly

memories from
past conflicts fought
of freedom for
dissenting thought

white pointed stars
on field of blue
stripes white and red
a symbol true

Independence Day

july the fourth
celebration
birthday party
for the nation

flags and buntings
red blue and white
stars beside stripes
a rousing sight

parades march by
little ones thrill
neighbors picnic
barbecues grill

watermelon
delicious fun
fireworks burst
when day is done

· 30 ·

Labor Day

when summertime
is almost done
a last chance for
some summer fun

picnics with food
and games to play
families spend
a happy day

at park or beach
or lake or pool
or backyard hose
to soak and cool

to honor those
who work for pay
a labor free
job holiday

· 32 ·

Constitution Day

united states
from revolution
governed now
by constitution

balanced powers
yield solutions
amendments guide
institutions

day seventeen
of september
special freedoms
we remember

a bill of rights
to keep us free
laws to protect
both you and me

·34·

Columbus Day

on the ocean
giant and blue
brave sailors left
the lands they knew

for distant worlds
beyond all known
ships farther than
seagulls had flown

upon far shores
new worlds revealed
land greater than
treasures could yield

a continent
with wonders new
plants and creatures
brave peoples too

· 36 ·

Veterans Day

to keep our country
safe and free
brave people serve
for you and me

on homeland and
on foreign shore
in peacetime and
in time of war

bold citizens
in loyalty
protect us and
our liberty

we honor those
alive and passed
whose constancy
remains steadfast

Thanksgiving Day

pilgrim people
from far away
came to this land
to live and pray

native people
taught them to sow
their seeds with fish
to help crops grow

together all
did celebrate
with harvest food
they shared and ate

we still give thanks
for food to eat
and for the things
that make life sweet

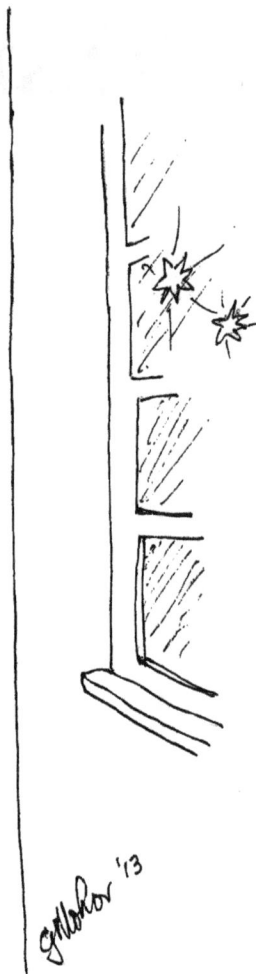

Christmas Day

pine needles green
winter frost white
crisp morning air
clear starry night

season's old songs
young faces bright
red ribbon bows
soft candle light

breakfast made hot
cocoa made sweet
wood fires warm
icy cold feet

families, friends
near and apart
memories stir
in every heart

SPECIAL DAYS

SUNDAY	MONDAY	TUESDAY	WEDNESDAY	THURSDAY	FRIDAY	SATURDAY
	1	2	3	4	5	6
7	8	9	10	11	12	13
14	15	16	17	18	19	20
21	22	23	24	25	26	27
28	29	30	31			

Written By: Alice L. Muhor

Illustrated by: Carol J. Muhor

Chapter Two

Other Observances

Mardi Gras

a carnival
with colors bold
bead strings of green
purple and gold

shrove tuesday meal
a pancake feast
made to use up
all fat and yeast

temptation we
now satisfy
tomorrow's wants
we will defy

so party on
all have a blast
then forty days
we long will fast

Chinese New Year

long ribbons dance
both left and right
to cut the air
with colors bright

when up and down
the ribbons flow
in circles high
and circles low

to lift and drop
and swing and sway
as ribbons dance
on new year's day

in pathways made
when ribbons twirl
to loop and turn
and curve and curl

Ground Hog Day

anxious people
eagerly wait
for a sign of
their weather fate

half way between
winter and spring
cloudy or bright
the crucial thing

if a shadow
the woodchuck cast
still six more weeks
of winter's blast

if a shadow
does not appear
an early spring
will soon be here

•50•

St. Valentine's Day

we celebrate
this special day
with candy treats
and words we say

a greeting card
painted pretty
with rhyming verse
sweet and witty

folded inside
an envelope
to be received
with joy we hope

a poem sent
to someone fine
i will be yours
will you be mine

·52·

St. Patrick's Day

march seventeenth
all claim to be
from irish stock
with green to see

of saint and elf
tall tales are told
from stories true
to legends bold

shamrock clovers
for three in one
or leprechauns
for blarney fun

from ancient land
proud people came
for work and lore
they now have fame

·54·

Dr. Seuss' Birthday

reading can be
a special gift
to give yourself
a happy lift

reading is more
than words we say
stories can take
you far away

reading can help
you to explore
what life was like
in times before

reading is how
we learn new ways
to do good things
in future days

· 56 ·

Vernal Equinox

a balance of
both dark and light
daytime lengthens
to equal night

the day we mark
once every year
in hope that spring
will soon appear

from underground
or planted seed
in flower fruit
or crop to feed

in blossom bright
with smell so sweet
for birds and bees
and bugs to eat

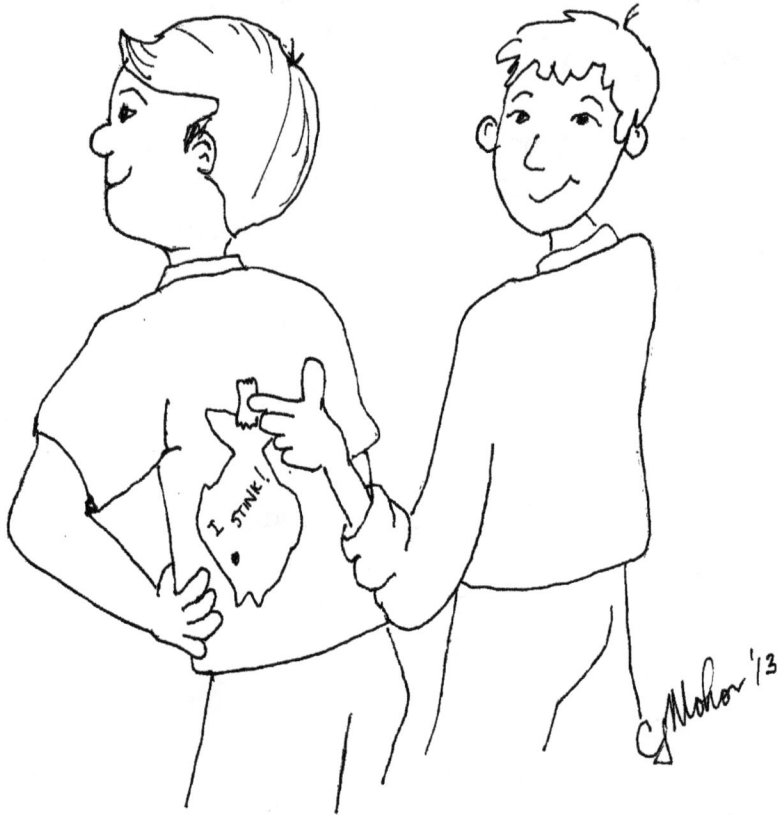

All Fools' Day

april the first
a special day
for silly fun
with jokes to play

honest people
say words untrue
to tease the likes
of me and you

to laugh out loud
when we obey
the foolish things
they do or say

a happy way
to celebrate
a season all
so long await

·60·

Earth Day

we remember
once every year
this planet earth
our mother dear

we need to show
our mother care
so we will have
enough clean air

with water clear
and sunlight bright
to grow our food
and give us light

we need our plants
for food and air
our world needs us
to show we care

Arbor Day

to plant a tree
is something grand
to give us shade
to sit or stand

but also to
help clean our air
for oxygen
for all to share

or to hold firm
our soil when
rain sleet or snow
fall down again

all people then
indeed agree
a wonder is
a growing tree

May Day

a special day
in times of old
to celebrate
the change from cold

with warmer days
and longer sun
children would do
a dance for fun

in a circle
with ribbons bright
dancers would curve
both left and right

to weave their way
around a pole
a pleasant way
to take a stroll

· 66 ·

Cinco de Mayo

our neighbors south
in mexico
recall a time
from long ago

when soldiers from
the country france
invaded and
did far advance

to overtake
an army small
of mexicans
who gave their all

to persevere
by desperate will
to resist far
beyond their skill

• 68 •

Summer Solstice

the longest day
with shortest night
begins a time
of brightest light

a season for
our crops to grow
and busy lives
to ease and slow

for rest beneath
tree branches wide
when lazy days
are spent outside

or splash and play
in water cool
on days away
from work or school

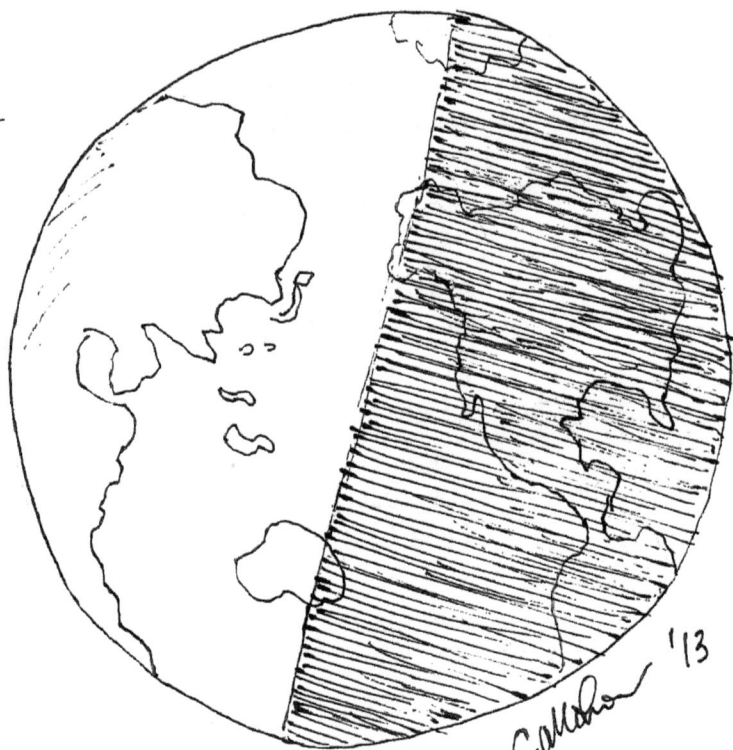

°70°

Autumnal Equinox

cool autumn nights
warm summer days
seasons respond
to nature's ways

a balance comes
to dark and light
as day retreats
to longer night

soon leaves will turn
to colors bold
as morning chills
turn nearer cold

as seasons change
all do prepare
for when the earth
will seem most bare

·72·

Halloween

harvest's reaping
corn stalks and hay
jack-o'-lanterns
to light the way

apples made sweet
fires lit bright
while restless souls
disturb the night

skeletons shake
as monsters roar
witches cackle
from door to door

ghosts and goblins
parade about
now trick or treat
the spirits shout

•74•

Saint Nicholas

when i was young
the church made me
a bishop near
a distant sea

a holy man
the people said
then far and wide
my fame was spread

i gave money
it has been told
for the needy
coins made of gold

good children still
can look for me
in shoe in sock
or under tree

Winter Solstice

ancient people
of northern lands
would ready for
winter's demands

of frigid cold
and drifts of snow
with wassail hot
and mistletoe

boughs evergreen
and carol song
with candles bright
the evening long

from shortest day
through longest night
a yule log burned
till morning light

Kwanzaa

time to recall
at end of year
principles for
folks living here

the heritage
of a proud race
from africa
the first birthplace

whose people share
their core values
with cultures of
assorted hues

to overcome
trial and strife
to celebrate
our common life

Written By: Alice L. Mohor

Illustrated by: Carol J. Mohor

Chapter Three

Special Days

· 82 ·

Ice Skating

in wintertime
on sheets of ice
skating outside
is always nice

when gliding on
thin blades of steel
your body has
a special feel

pushing along
as muscles pump
speeding up for
a leap or jump

straining to win
a friendly race
or spinning with
control and grace

Sledding

sledding on snow
a certain thrill
sliding all day
down a tall hill

a running start
then belly flop
careening to
a sudden stop

or riding down
a backyard run
time and again
till day is done

then inside for
hot cocoa sweet
with marshmallows
a winter treat

Winter Rain

though gloomy days
can be a drain
we celebrate
our winter rain

and are consoled
when we recall
the summer droughts
that can befall

our garden plants
and grassy lawns
when everyday
a hot sun dawns

to dry the land
and drain the lake
to heat the air
from warm to bake

March

all night and day
a cold wind blew
southland winter
is not yet through

but tomorrow
we may feel warm
unless of course
gray storm clouds form

to block the sun
and loose the rain
we know we need
but still complain

because we are
so anxious for
the joys that spring
will soon restore

· 90 ·

Springtime

springtime is here
flowers in bloom
bright colors seen
outside my room

the mornings cool
but noontimes warm
birds build their nests
honeybees swarm

afternoons bright
with evenings long
chirping crickets
call a night song

tree blossoms float
from high above
all seen a gift
sent here with love

Blackberry Winter

when spring is late
or fall too soon
the world it seems
is out of tune

but early spring
a welcome treat
that people cheer
and thrill to greet

so nature's trick
of winter cold
after a time
of blossoms bold

will chill the feet
and try the heart
once warmer days
of springtime start

· 94 ·

Spring Rain

rain that returns
day after day
limits the choice
of how you play

feeling confined
bored you may shout
rain go away
let me go out

remembering
all plants need rain
stop to look through
a window pane

notice the view
outside your room
the wonder of
flowers in bloom

An Outside Walk

when i go out
to take a walk
it's also nice
to share a talk

with an old friend
or someone new
to learn about
our points of view

and exercise
our bodies well
while we listen
and while we tell

as we proceed
along our way
to revel in
another day

Commencement

graduation
oh happy day
congratulations
we do say

from nursery
to college bound
once small now big
time goes around

ahead for you
more joy but still
not many things
will top this thrill

blessings as you
progress in life
with laughter large
and little strife

· 100 ·

Triumphs

to pump a swing
was sheer delight
when motion would
thrill and excite

to hang by knees
from bar or tree
made upside down
a thing to see

to balance on
bicycle tires
was once the height
of my desires

to learn to swim
and relax fear
a summer joy
i still hold dear

• 102 •

Heat

though summer days
are very hot
with heavy air
and bugs to swat

there still are things
most opportune
like reading in
the afternoon

because it is
too hot to play
we must relax
for most the day

to keep ourselves
out of the sun
we stay inside
for quiet fun

•104•

Summer Rain

when summer days
are very hot
and outdoor play
almost forgot

our tolerance
for time spent in
may finally
begin to thin

but sudden rain
that cools the air
will also wash
away despair

when children run
outside to dash
through puddles made
to kick and splash

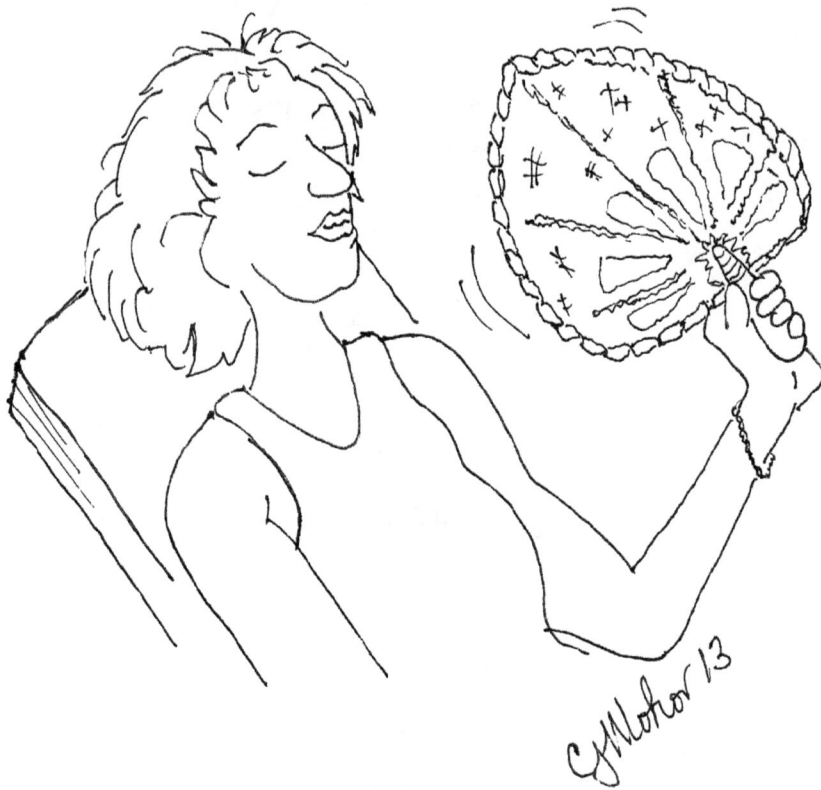

· 106 ·

August

all thirty one
are special days
but august has
no holidays

hot sticky heat
hours of light
sunshine beaming
white hot and bright

summer season
past half way done
but time still left
for lazy fun

vacations far
or weekends near
long august days
are always dear

· 108 ·

An August Treat

though people may
unkind berate
new jersey is
the garden state

the produce in
the summertime
is grown close by
with taste sublime

from farmers' fields
each road side stand
with local food
is in demand

and when at last
white corn is sweet
it is so good
to cook and eat

· 110 ·

Taken Back

at summer camp
in new york state
autumn did not
patiently wait

before we packed
to leave for school
the mountain air
would start to cool

now in the south
of scorching sun
summer is not
so quickly done

but with the chill
of early dawn
i think again
of time now gone

° ||| °

· 112 ·

Indian Summer

a brief return
to summer heat
can be for some
a welcome treat

a change of pace
from winter bound
after a frost
upon the ground

a short reprieve
for outside fun
or time to get
more yard work done

but summer haze
will disappear
when autumn does
again appear

· 114 ·

Autumn

before the leaves
fall on the ground
a wonderment
does all surround

as colors change
from summer green
to paint each tree
an autumn scene

of flaming red
or yellow gold
or orange bright
to then behold

a beauty that
will take a rest
when winter's cold
becomes our guest

Turkey Dinner

holiday feast
a tasty treat
favorite foods
we love to eat

a turkey stuffed
and roasted brown
with gravy fine
the best in town

from vegetables
to pumpkin pie
our meal complete
content we sigh

after today
tomorrow's thrill
leftover meals
are better still

Overnight

late in the fall
before the snow
to grandmom's house
we kids would go

together all
would try to sleep
quiet sometimes
too hard to keep

in the morning
with old clothes on
outside raking
to clear the lawn

with bedspread full
alley to curb
leaves carried to
a pile superb

· 120 ·

A Party

when people join
to have some fun
after a day
of hard work done

they gather 'round
with food to eat
and visit with
the friends they meet

then when they hear
good music play
they soon begin
to swing and sway

and delight in
the time they share
away from stress
away from care

Happy Birthday

a birthday is
a special day
for dear ones all
to shout hooray

to recognize
and celebrate
or lovingly
humiliate

with words of cheer
or words of woe
for memories
from long ago

children at heart
all long to hear
happy birthday
said every year

Written By: Alice L. Mohor   Illustrated by: Carol J. Mohor

Chapter Four

Religious Holidays

Passover

families in
celebration
join to recall
liberation

an ancient tale
each year retold
how god released
a pharaoh's hold

with famine plague
and pestilence
his power was
beyond defense

from slavery
they won release
to find a place
to live in peace

Easter

this time each spring
we celebrate
the son of man
who conquered hate

a life of fear
held all at bay
until he came
to lead the way

from separate
to love for all
beyond a death
with bitter gall

his risen life
inspired those
who spread good news
to friends and foes

·130·

Rosh Hashanah

time to worship
to think to pray
sunset begins
each holy day

faithful people
listen to hear
a ram horn blast
for the new year

into waters
flowing past swift
the old year's sins
are cast adrift

honey apples
a special treat
so days ahead
are extra sweet

Yom Kippur

a day to fast
a day to pray
time to repent
sorrys to say

a day to ask
forgiveness for
the sins we made
the year before

time to reflect
a day to think
no work or play
no food or drink

one last attempt
to make amends
time to be right
with god and friends

Harvest Festival

a harvest moon
tribes together
join in thanks for
growing weather

the winds move in
a circle round
while up and down
the grinders pound

the winds then lift
the grinded corn
to the spirit
the grain is born

native people
we dance to pray
to celebrate
our gifts today

°135°

Diwali

awareness of
an inner light
to live a life
both good and right

a festival
of noise and lights
five special days
four special nights

lanterns and lamps
to guide the way
while fireworks
chase bad away

a peace beyond
knowledge astute
awakened by
earnest pursuit

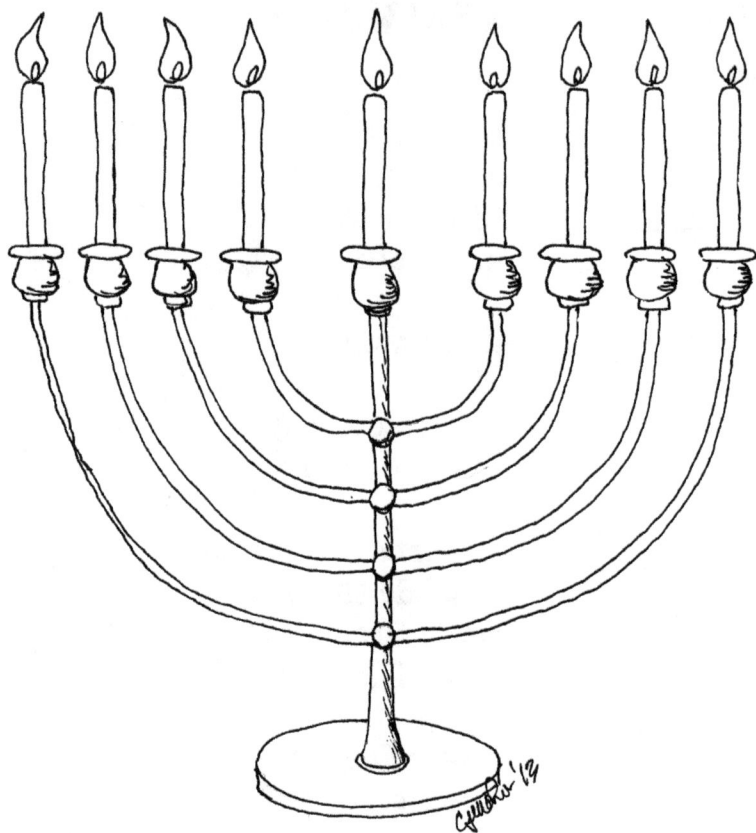

•138•

Hanukkah

a festival
of candle lights
to remember
eight special nights

when ancient lamps
molded from clay
with oil enough
to burn one day

kindled a flame
beyond supply
as if the fuel
did multiply

to dedicate
the temple won
when foreign rule
had been undone

•140•

Christmas

we celebrate
a time long past
the birth of christ
that was forecast

conquered people
prayed for relief
a coming king
was their belief

a messiah
to set them free
from foreign rule
and tyranny

a soldier not
but simple boy
who grew to teach
god's love and joy

°142°

Ramadan

for ramadan
once every year
devout muslims
with faith adhere

to fast a month
from dawn each day
till sunset when
all eat and pray

refraining from
both food and drink
reminds us of
our need to think

of life in tune
with one's belief
and offerings
for poor relief

•144•

Eid al-Fitr

charity first
for those with less
united with
all who profess

islamic faith
and do adhere
to disciplines
made very clear

a festive meal
after a prayer
with food enough
for all to share

to celebrate
ramadan's end
adherents feast
with kin and friend

· 146 ·

Eid al-Adha

in the twelfth month
on the tenth day
the end of hajj
a holiday

to celebrate
four happy days
a festival
of thanks and praise

grateful people
will share their feast
gifts are given
to those with least

families friends
and neighbors too
remember all
that god can do

Alice Louise Mohor began writing rhyming poetry for her elementary physical education students. In addition to writing about movement principles and concepts, Alice wrote poetry for other school subject areas. Although retired from teaching, Alice continues to write and share her poetry with children and adults.

Carol Jean Mohor's interest in art began with her desire to learn how to draw the characters in Charles Schultz's *Peanuts* cartoons. Since retiring from teaching elementary art full-time, Carol continues to teach art part-time, chair her state retired art educators' association division and co-chair an international airport's youth art gallery.

www.ingramcontent.com/pod-product-compliance
Lightning Source LLC
Chambersburg PA
CBHW050639150426
42813CB00054B/1112